BUT FIRST
We Live

Poems of Trials, Trails, and Healing Through Nature

Inez Nambangi

But First We Live: Poems of Trials, Trails, and Healing Through Nature
© copyright 2025 by Inez Nambangi. All rights reserved. No part of this book may be reproduced in any form whatsoever, by photography or xerography or by any other means, by broadcast or transmission, by translation into any kind of language, nor by recording electronically or otherwise, without permission in writing from the author, except by a reviewer, who may quote brief passages in critical articles or reviews.

ISBN 13: 979-8-9920774-2-1
Library of Congress Catalog Number: 2025908830
Printed in the United States of America
First Printing: 2025
28 27 26 25 25   5 4 3 2 1

Illustrated by Megan Rizzo, DaisyIllustrations.com
Cover and interior design by Ngân Huỳnh

Wise Ink
PO Box 580195
Minneapolis, MN 55458-0195
www.WiseInk.com

Wise Ink is a creative publishing agency for game-changers. Wise Ink authors uplift, inspire, and inform, and their titles support building a better and more equitable world. For more information, visit WiseInk.com.

Dedication

To my daughters, Lisa and Jasmine. May the light I shine on their lives help them forge new exciting paths as they, in turn, illumine the world for those who will come after.

Table of Contents

This Trail I've Walked 1
Face Your Demons 4
Out of the Forlorn Meadow 6
This Day, Too, Will Be Done 9
Good Fortune Is Just That 11
Reflections 14
Tam-Tam, Heartbeat, Tam-Tam 18
How the Voices Scream 24
Slay 27
Gursha 30
I Didn't Know Her, I Didn't Need To 33
Survival Street 35
What the Bird Teaches Me About Soaring 38
We Believe You 40
Thunder Bay Park 42
We See You 44
Let the Light In 46
Girl Meets Woman 49
And When Faced with Fear 52
Waiting Out the Winter 54

Decide to Forge Your Own Way	58
Where I Belong	60
Superwomen	62
Reclaim Your Power	65
The Walk to Freedom	68
Make Your Heart Whole Again	69
The Loudest Silence	71
An Invitation	73
O My Soul	75
Broken Yet Whole	77
Presenting: Me	79
Finding the Mountaintop	82
Out of Darkness	85
All Hurt the Same	87
Cocoon	89
Your Garden, Your Shears	91
Symphony of a Million Leaves	93
An Ode to Nature	95
Darkish Thoughts	97
A Recipe for Renewal	100
The Sword over My Head	102
On Contemplating Joy	104
We Will Be Glorious Again	106
The Raging Fire of Hope	107
Happy Women's Day?	109
Transform	112
What Was and What Will Be	114
Shadows	116
You Will Thrive!	118
Blessings in Stillness	120

Change Your Story	122
Fears Are Just Memories	124
Women the World Forgot	126
Castaway	128
Love Is Life Itself	130
About the Author and Illustrator	133

If you grew up in an abusive home, please be intentional in seeking healing. This is the only way to shame your abusers and free yourself. Abuse is not a "generational curse"; it is learned behavior. You cannot afford to imitate the behaviors that robbed you of joy and dignity and basic human freedom. If you didn't deserve to suffer that, what makes it right for you to turn around and become an abuser? Why do you think it is right for YOUR victims to suffer the same fate? Why punish unsuspecting people for something that has nothing to do with them?

We will no longer be silent. We will talk, we will shout. We say NO to domestic abuse.

THIS TRAIL I'VE WALKED

If I ever write my memoirs
This trail will be prominent as the place where I met and discovered and accepted and loved myself
I escape from a vibrant house to this space
Where I again escape into my thoughts
And yet . . .
I remain aware of the wonders of nature that surround me
I have uncovered my truth on this trail.
I own it, I speak it and live it daily. No apologies.
I am forthright about who I am and what I want from life. Take it or leave it.
On this trail
I have laughed and cried
I have loved and lost
I have sought and found
I have feared and conquered
I have hurt and healed
I have learned how to live my best life
I have learned that regret is a time waster
I have learned that I hate no one
I have learned that I am made strong and whole and bold by my brokenness
I have learned that I am perfectly imperfect

I have learned to accept an apology that was never made
I have found peace profound
I have discovered the giant in me
And yet...
I have come to terms with how little I am compared to the glorious nature around me
And yet...
I have discovered how precious and significant my place in the cosmos is!
On this trail
I live and learn and grow and THRIVE!
My name is Inez, Woman, Introvert, Daughter, Sister, Lover, Friend, Aunt, Mother of Two and then some.
I am ENOUGH
If I ever write my memoirs...
Thank you, Maplewood Parks

Face Your Demons

We all have them.
They terrify you
They steal your joy
They imprison you
It is that which you fear
It is that which you do not speak of
It is that which you speak of with fear
And trembling
It is that which you think you need but
It kills you slowly but surely
It is that which you hide from
It is that thing that stunts your growth
And makes you fear the dawn of a new day
And every approaching night
And leads you to habits that you think
Help you cope
But instead you sink
Deeper
And deeper
And deeper still
It is mostly in the form of a person
One who should nurture you
But instead they hurt you

And steal your dignity
Your peace of mind
Your joy
Sometimes that demon is a thing
Sometimes, rarely . . . but yes . . . sometimes
You have the power to get rid of this demon
Look it in the face
Summon that strength that is in you
The strength that is inherent in every human
Look this monster in the face and say
ENOUGH!
For my birthday this year, I wish you
PEACE!

Out of the Forlorn Meadow

And a chance to retreat
Into my mind
Instead, I find myself snapping away
And writing down a few lines . . .
I seem to do that
A lot in recent times
It is a cold Minnesota evening
But who wants to stay indoors
When you can have this amazing time with nature?
And then it hit me:
There are just a few birds still chirping in the woods
The once-lush meadows now look forlorn
Adieu beautiful flowers!
I stopped and smelled you
Throughout the summer!
Now you, too, are but a memory
My walking buddies, too,
Are nowhere to be found
No dogs yapping
And snapping me back into reality
As I walk past the playground
That, too, is desolate
There are no children squealing in delight

As they chase each other round and around . . .
The basketball hoop
Looks like a sad relic from summers past
I tarry for a minute, lost in thought
Thinking how beautiful this was
Just a few weeks ago!
But snap!
This IS beautiful!
It all depends on what you seek!
This is indeed glorious
And its magic is in the certainty
That it will return to its former beauty
Almost effortlessly
In just a few months!
That might be the whole point!
If it is breathtakingly beautiful all the time
Where is its mystery?
We need to lose it from time to time
So when it returns
It takes our breath away all over again
And we wonder at its majesty
The mystery of nature!
In its rebirth
We are rebirthed!
This is the miracle of life!
This gives me hope:
No matter how bleak things look right now
If you give it time
All will be well again
You have to stand up

Don't roll over
Stand UP!
Stick to your guns
Fight. Fight. Fight!
On this cold November evening
In the city of Maplewood
I am reassured . . .
On my birthday this year
I bring you HOPE
You will THRIVE!

This Day, Too, Will Be Done

Time for a morning walk
Some ice on the track
But still a beautiful day
To be outdoors enjoying nature
Oh what a glorious day!
Scared of the cold and the snow?
Nah, we know better
We got this!
There's nothing to fear
Instead, we enjoy!
I wish a day like this
Would last a little longer
Than its allotted twenty-four hours!
But alas!
This day, too, will be done
And we always hope for
A better tomorrow
But why wait for tomorrow?
Take advantage of each day
Make some awesome memories
Store them in your soul
No joy is too small
While we have today

Let's make the best of it!
Even in your trials
Find something to enjoy in each day!
Life is made of moments
Enjoy the good ones
Get strength from the bad ones
Look for something to celebrate
And you'll find it
On my birthday this year
I wish you Moments such as this ♥

Good Fortune Is Just That

I take nothing for granted!
Not my health
Not even my good fortune
For it is just that:
Good fortune
I am not more deserving
Than any other human
I do not take it for granted!
Not my children
I brought these two into the world
In spite of my own humanness
I know science might explain it
I am no scientist
I still frankly cannot begin to fathom
The miracle that is
The whole process of procreation
I do not need to understand it
I am humbled and thankful
For the chance to partake
In something of such magnitude!
Something so magical
That is beyond my comprehension
I do not take them for granted!

I do not take love for granted
For I know not
The sacrifices you willingly make
To make yourself, your heart available to me
I do not understand the extent to which
My shortcomings affect you
And yet you are unwavering
How could I ever take such
Sacrificial love for granted?
I do not take my family for granted
Such an amazing lot
Who did not choose me
Nor did I choose them
It was ordained by a higher power
That we would walk together
I am eternally thankful
I do not take my friendships for granted
How can I?
There are so many you could choose
Yet you chose me
How can I take you for granted?
I certainly do not take my foes for granted
I pray I have none
If I do . . . nah, I don't
And yet . . .
If I do have foes
How can I take them for granted
When I know not the source or depth
Of their angst?
I'll practice patience

And kindness
And understanding
Because I might learn something of value
I take no one and nothing for granted
How could one take anything
That is so beyond human comprehension for granted?
Something that is so intricately crafted
So ingeniously engineered
So mysterious
So precious
So glorious
The depths of which are unfathomable
How can I take anything for granted?
I take nothing for granted!
Forever grateful
For my birthday this year
I wish you clarity

REFLECTIONS

Reflections come at you
When least expected
They come to you
In all colors
I usually like what I see
When I behold
My reflection
I love it!
Usually beautiful
Appealing
Attractive
Amazing!
Sometimes I drool over my reflection
Other times I can't deal
I close my eyes
I look away
Because
Doubts set in
I'm too curvy
I'm not curvy enough
Too petite
Not petite enough
Very beautiful

Not beautiful enough
Too busty
Not busty enough
Need a boob job
No, you're a whack job
A true kaleidoscope
And this is on my good days!
On my better days
I hardly see the details
In the physical
I look past that into the spiritual
And have different reflections
Am I kind enough
Am I gentle enough
Am I loving enough
Am I forgiving enough
Have I found my purpose
Am I fulfilling said purpose
I love my reflections
Both my insecurities and confidence
They keep me grounded
They keep me humble
And reminded of one fact:
I'm a work in progress
I never want to be too confident
Or I'll stop trying
I love them
Both physical and spiritual
My reflections
My perfect imperfections

That could get better
I will never be the most amazing
The smartest
Or the most beautiful
But one thing is sure
I'm the best me
The most me
The only me!
Better at being me than anyone else
Another thing is sure:
I could be better
I love my reflections
The physical and spiritual
They make me who I am
How about you
Have you checked out your reflections lately?
Are they comforting or frightening
Are they cringeworthy or praiseworthy?
For my birthday this year
I wish you worthy reflections

Tam-Tam, Heartbeat, Tam-Tam

Music speaks to my heart
And soul
Soul Makossa
The Bikutsi
The Afrobeat
Reggae, Blues, Jazz
I love it all
But the sound of the tam-tam!
Now that stops me in my tracks
Wakes me up
And takes me back
To a time before time existed
It is the sound
That's native to my soul
The sound that reminds me
Of community
Of love
And passion!
It starts slowly, gently, softly
Almost hesitant
Tamtam-tamtam-tamtam
It builds up slowly
With the kinfolk

Dancing
Gyrating
Grooving
Swaying from side to side
Tap-tapping
To the rhythm of the tam-tam
It builds up slowly still
Tatatata-tatatata
We dance with more vigor
And then it reaches crescendo!
Tatatatatatata
And the dancing becomes wild
Almost out of control
Everyone doing their own thing
As endowed as we are
In all the right places . . .
This quickly becomes a sight to behold
A sensual celebration
Exquisite!
A frenzy!
Freestyle
Each doing their own thing
As the tam-tam has a different message
For each one
Body and spirit become one
Nothing else exists in that moment
Nothing else matters
Except the music
The dancer
And the spirit

The spirit completely takes over
Time itself stands still
Man and the universe become one
In that moment
Trancelike!
You don't want this dance to end
Ever
But then, with a jolt
Reality returns
Mbana Loba!*
Nostalgia
For my birthday this year, I wish you a reconnection with your innermost self

---

* Cameroonian language. It means "Dear God!" or "I swear to God!"

How the Voices Scream

Too many voices in the DARK
Uncertain about what they say
But say something they must
You don't belong here, they say
You don't sound like us
Why did you come here
What's wrong with your own world
And yet you THRIVE
You speak with an accent
You can't speak English
We don't understand you
You are too dark
You don't belong here
Please go back home
And yet
You THRIVE
Your customs are primitive
You're not Christian
Or not Christian enough
You are savages
You have no roads
You are disease-ridden
You live in trees

And still you THRIVE
You are unclean
You smell
Don't touch me
Don't look at me
Go back home!
And BOOM you THRIVE
We are building a wall
You will build the wall
We have built the wall
We will keep you out
You want to respond
Hey, hold up!
Why are you able to come to my world
Own half the land
Own my government
Pillage my world
Make use of my resources
Use up the last drop
Leave nothing for me
Drop your chemical waste
Kill my people
Turn them into lab rats
Kill them some more
Come in at will
As frequently as you will
Why is it okay for you to do this?
And yet I am not welcome here
Because I'm different
When you come to my world

Are you not different?
Do you speak my language?
Can you speak it without an accent?
What makes you so special
Why are there rules for me
And none for you?
Forget it, I say
Don't engage them
They are not interested in your logic
They can't hear you
They won't hear you
They don't see you
All they see is your color
Just do your thing
Today you are in Texas
Tomorrow it will be London
Or Paris
Or Abidjan
Or Libreville
Still
You will THRIVE and shine!
Find fertile land and bloom
Wherever you find yourself
The world belongs to us ALL
For my birthday this year, I pray you THRIVE

Slay

Social media's phenomenon
Of slay kings and queens
Has us mesmerized daily
As we drool over images
Beyond beautiful
We wonder at how they
Slay so effortlessly
As we gawk
We can't help
But imagine the slayers we are missing
What lies ahead for future generations
Where are the dragon slayers of our day . . .
Our world is ravaged
By the effects of wars past
And present
Yet we are trying our best to start more
Someone please slay that
Political crisis all over Africa
Are we slaying that?
Bloodshed all over the world
Wherever humans find themselves
Who's slaying that
Our society is rife with corruption

Who will slay that?
Genocide . . . genocide . . . genocide
I'm begging you, slay that
Child trafficking is the order of the day
Why don't you slay that?
Racial discrimination
Who's slaying that?
Homelessness everywhere you look
Can't we slay that?
Poverty swallowing up communities
Are we slaying that?
Child abuse
For crying out loud
If there's only one thing you can slay
Let it be that
Domestic abuse
Are you really waiting for someone
To slay that for you?
Please slay that dastardly dragon yourself
Or it'll eat you up
Alcoholism
Won't you help slay that?
Drug abuse
Are we even trying to slay that?
Don't we see what it is doing
To the human race
Will you please slay that?
Slay kings and queens
You slay us
But we are not the ones who need slaying

Have you slayed any dragons lately?
For my birthday this year
I wish you the courage to
Stand up against social ills
Slay that!

GURSHA

With a rolling R
Amongst the people of Ethiopia
And beyond
A culture of love
And caring
And trust
Amongst friends or family
Nonromantic love
Or romantic love
Simply: love
Free for all
Endearing and enduring
A piece of the fabric
Included in the tapestry
Of love and kindness
Intricately woven into
The consciousness of a people
That which defines their cultural heritage
Gursha
With the fingers
You scoop a bite of food into
A loved one's mouth
Before feeding yourself

You delay your own gratification
To meet their need first
Sacrificial love!
Gursha
You care for the other
Before caring for yourself
You feed the other
Before nourishing yourself
As if to say
You matter
You are important
I value you
I am because you are
Strong communities are built
When we recognize
The importance of community
When the lives and well-being
Of all matter
When the needs of others
Are uppermost in our minds
When the lives and comfort of others
Are prioritized
As we seem to forget
What unites us
As brother turns against brother
And sister against sister
May we remember
The spirit of love
That holds us together
May the culture of Gursha pervade

All areas of our lives
So we are again conscious
Of that which unites us
So we remember that we are a unit
Stronger together
Gursha!

I Didn't Know Her, I Didn't Need To

Lost her life this week
To domestic violence
As we speak
A sister is losing herself
To domestic abuse!
I don't know her
I didn't know her
And yet I know her
I feel her pain
I mourn her loss
Because of our shared humanity
Because of our shared womanhood
Because of our shared sisterhood
I hear her cries
Because of the pressure placed on us
By society
To endure
I know her!
And now I beseech all who remain
All who struggle
Know that you got this

Know that the power to end this
Resides in you
Know that violence is not the way
Know that you have the strength
The wherewithal to say
No more!
Know that you have a sound mind
Use it!
Know that you have a beautiful life
Live it!
You can take that walk
To freedom
It starts from the mind
Be determined
And then start walking
And be free
So you can soar
And experience life

SURVIVAL STREET

Light snow on the ground today
I step out in my walking gear and spirit
As I have thoughts that need to be thought
But behold, it is snowing
Therefore treacherous terrain
For the snow makes it slippery
But see, these thoughts need to be thunk
So walk I must
But as soon as I start walking
My survival instinct kicks in
And I am on Survival Street
As I must concentrate and be sure
Each step lands on solid ground
I do not notice any of the things that usually
Bring me joy
Not the birds' nests
Or the snow-covered trees
Not the half-frozen lake
Not even the beautiful houses I walk past
Nor the once-grassy knolls
Now covered in snow
I do, however, hear the sound of the falling snow
And the distant hum of car engines

My apologies, Greta
I know the harm
the fumes wreak on our environment
But the sound is soothing
Again, my sincere apologies
I enjoy these sounds while walking
Carefully, not carefree like I usually do
My thoughts flee as even they realize
I am now on Survival Street
I tell myself *this is it*
This is what happens to you
When you spend years living in survival mode
Life goes past you
You miss opportunities
You lose loved ones
You lose your support system
You lose your connections
You lose yourself
Because you are trying to survive
The next attack
The next danger
The next assault
This constant strife is your world
It is your reality
Whatever you do
Please do not lose yourself
That is damnation!
To be victorious, you have to fight!
I know
I've been there

Some people get out
Some do not realize they have the power
To get out
They resign themselves
To what they think is their fate
This is not your fate
You can reshape the future if you so desire
Otherwise
This Survival Street will steal your future
If you don't get away from there
Shut it down!
Don't close it for reconstruction
Shut it down and throw away the key
Do not ever return there
It is a dead end
A death trap!
Go! Move! Leave
Yes, leave to live life to the fullest
Much love, from my heart to yours

What the Bird Teaches Me About Soaring

Saw a bird in flight
On my walk this morning
Took what I thought was a great shot
Checked my camera
Nothing
Was not disappointed
Because the thought it evoked
Remained
Watching a bird in flight
Is my definition of freedom
They have challenges too
They are living creatures, after all
But that moment when they don't even need to flap
That moment when they just seem to float
They seem to experience complete freedom
At least from my human eye
Blissful
They seem to soar left and then right
Effortlessly!
They have flapped enough to pick up speed
And then they simply float

What is holding you down?
What is stopping you from progress?
What is cheating you of your freedom?
Start flapping
You will become strong
Don't stop flapping
Stick to your goal
Soon you will take flight
And experience the freedom you deserve
There is a time for flapping
There is a time for soaring
Soar in power!

We Believe You

I believe you
I understand your pain
How do you want to proceed
And how can I support you
The best words of support ever uttered
At the same time they validate
They let you know you are not alone
And they offer a hand to hold
They let you know the decision is yours
They offer help through the journey ahead
You alone can walk your journey
But these supporters illumine your way
Along your path
They do not condemn
They do not advise
They do not judge
They do not blame
And dear Lord, the blame!
They never say *what did you do to cause this*
They never say *why don't you persevere*
They never say *maybe if you obeyed*
They never ever say *what will people say*
They never say *remember our culture*

When good people know you need help
When they know you need healing
When they know you are fighting for your life
They know
You are their focus
Not the one that causes you pain
Not tradition
Not culture
YOU are the focus
They cry with you
They hug you
They give you strength
They whisper life-giving words
You can do this
Thank you Lola* and the sisterhood of women
Who know what support looks like

---

* Lola Omolola is the founder of Female In, a Facebook support group for women.

THUNDER BAY PARK

As I walk down Thunder Bay Park this morning
I can tell my step is lighter than usual
I feel a certain change in my spirit
A change in my world
I think the universe shifted in that moment
And I think to myself
I wonder what burden just got lifted
I dwell on it some more and realize
It was a surge of joy
Joy because I am here
I survived all that was ever thrown at me
Joyful for my support system
Firmly behind me
And around me
Joyful because I see the world around me
In beautiful colors
Joy because I know even those who now struggle
Will overcome
Reach out to someone for support
They will give you strength when you are weak
There is no shame in that
There is no shame in being a victim
There is no shame in asking for help

Fight!
Don't give up!
You'll get there
But first you fight for your life
The day will come when you'll say
Oh what joy!
Glorious!

WE SEE YOU

Walked past a woman and her dog on my walk yesterday
Or was it the day before
She did not have a smile
And I didn't give her one of mine
Instead, I dwelled on the fact that
She avoided my gaze
Why did that matter?
In a moment of weakness
I failed to see what matters
The woman, not her appearance, should matter
I should have given her one sing-song
Good mor . . . ning
She would have looked up
She would have looked at me
And I would have followed up with a smile
A dazzling smile
She might have smiled back
That might have brightened her day
It might have helped improve her mood
Her smile would have released dopamine
She would have felt a surge of joy
Her day would have been brightened
She might have paid that smile forward

So many people would have been affected
By that one smile
Had I given it to her
But no, I had to be petty
And wonder why she avoided my gaze
I'll do better next time
I must brighten my corner of the world
I must put the needs of other people first
Not their outward appearance
I must not try to know
Why they avoid eye contact
That is neither here nor there
I must offer a kind word
A warm smile
They will know they matter
They are not invisible
I see them
We see them
They are not alone
I must help them heal emotionally
Every gesture counts
Every act of kindness
Is potentially lifesaving

LET THE LIGHT IN

Twenty-four degrees
Cold morning for a walk
But never too cold for these parts
Nothing is ever too cold here
Even at subzero
Trudging through the snow in some parts
Feeling quite cold and a little hesitant
Almost defeated
Too cold
Even a little gloomy
But then the sun bursts through
Changing everything
With it comes joy
And hope
And warmth
And light
It is still twenty-four degrees
Sunshine changes the landscape
Both within and without
The negative feelings dissipate
Giving way to unbridled joy
It is a great day for a walk!
This is true of human situations

We think our situation is shameful
We don't want anyone to find out
That which imprisons us
It is not our shame, but we know no better
Our struggles get worse
We have taken a vow of silence
We don't say a word
It gets worse
It festers
It consumes us
Yet we are silent
We think this is bravery
We guard the secret with our lives
Literally!
No one must know
It starts to choke us
We struggle to breathe
To survive
It is killing us
And yet we are resolved to be silent
We feel saintly
This suffering was preordained
It is my lot
I can do naught
To show my strength, I must endure
And then one day
We throw caution to the wind
Because there comes that day
When the mind decides it is time to unburden
Time to fight

Time to heal
We open the doors
The windows too
We let in the light
We expose the secret
We unburden
We let in more light
In the darkest crevices
Light chases out the darkness
And slowly but surely, we are stronger
Evil loses its power over us
It loses its grip
It is defeated
We get stronger still
We live and breathe and heal
We THRIVE
On this cold Thanksgiving morning
I pray you let in the light

GIRL MEETS WOMAN

Strange encounter today
As I take a walk
Sometimes brisk, sometimes leisurely
Suddenly, my mind is conjuring images
That don't seem possible
It's an encounter with my younger me
Quite an interesting exchange ensues
Younger me wonders
How did you become this woman
How do you have so much joy
How can you be so playful
And yet be so strong
So quiet and yet so loud
How can you be so happy when everything seems to crumble
After all the pain
All the scars
The struggles
The fights
The sheer impossibility
After all I went through
I could have sworn you would never emerge
How did you do it
The older me responds

Thanks to your resilience
Your sheer willpower
Your resourcefulness
Your refusal to give up
Thank you for the strength
In the face of adversity
Thank you for the courage to laugh
When you felt like crying
Thank you for staying steadfast
For the knowledge and belief
That eventually darkness gives way to light
That you can fight and win
That no giant is too big
When you have clean hands
Thank you for recognizing
The path of least resistance is a mirage
Thank you for all the scars
They are proof of the struggles
Because you were steadfast
Because you were resolute
And resilient
And fierce
Because you did not stop
Because you did not roll over
And give in to the pain
And hopelessness
And helplessness
Because you stayed strong
Eyes focused on the goal
Resolved never to give up your power

— Inez Nambangi —

Determined to fulfill your purpose
You paved the way for me
You went through fire
So I could be refined
You survived
I EMERGED!
Glory!

And When Faced with Fear

Pounding the pavement this morning
Walking away from a past
Not meant for me
The further I walk
The more time I have to process my thoughts
I have learned that thinking about it
Takes away its power
Now I look back and smile
And I know
That the adversity made me stronger
It catapulted me
Toward a beautiful future
Filled with possibilities
And the freedom
To be
To feel
To speak and LIVE
The things we take for granted!
If only we knew
The things that lurk in the dark
May we never dwell there again
Today I encourage you to face your fears
Don't cower

Don't pretend they don't exist
Don't hide it
Expose it!
Never think they are too much for you
Don't underestimate yourself
You are stronger than you know
Don't wait for someone to fight for you
Sometimes you're all you've got
You can do this yourself
And win
And live your best life!
Live life to the fullest!

Waiting Out the Winter

Of all the seasons
Winter is the harshest
By my estimation
Temperatures drop to below freezing
How tempting it would be
To stay indoors
And hibernate
Until the spring
But no
We turn it into fun
By walking
Ice fishing
Skiing
And ice-skating
We take the approach
Of finding the silver lining
And many come to love winter
In like manner
We have adversities in life
We don't hide
We don't give up
And surrender
Instead, we fight

Decide to Forge Your Own Way

More of a trudge than a leisurely walk
As I struggle with the snow this morning
Walk this path every day
With noticeable differences daily
Hard pushing through snow
Seven inches deep
Tried to make it easier
Stepped into the footprints in the snow
Of the guy who was there before
Not a good idea
The walker before me had long strides
Trying to use his footprints
Could have gone south . . .
I decide to forge my own way
Short, sure strides
Calves hurting from the effort
But sure enough
It got easier
Felt surer
Less painful
Met my goal
This morning
I am reminded of the need to pave my own way

My purpose
And my plan
And my resources
Are unique to me

Where I Belong

Amazing morning!
New beginnings
New day
New year
New decade!
Brand-new life
Awesome opportunities
Got up to love, music, and dance!
Put in an hour-long walk
Stopped frequently to marvel at nature
Too cold to smell the roses
So marveling, feeling, and gazing it is
Gazed at the snow adorning the trees like flowers
Felt the plush carpeting
Formed by the seven-inch-deep snow
That welcomes my every step
I breathe in the cold air that seems to warm me up
And energize me
And make me want more
Eventually turn around
Take a leisurely walk back home
Make it last as long as I can
The smell of candles

The sound of music
The delightful sounds of the children
Welcome me back into my warm loving home
Realize I love being outside
With the same fervor
That I love being at home
And I say to myself
This is where I want to be
This is where I belong
To love and be loved
To heal and be healed
To feel and be thankful
And to remember
That adversity doesn't last forever
To remember that kindness matters
To remember that I am because you are
And remember to make a positive impact daily
From my little corner of the world
This is why I'm here
Blessed assurance!
On this very cold day
In the city of Maplewood
I wish you a season full of joy and love and laughter and life!

SUPERWOMEN

Every Superwoman
I encounter reminds me
Of every last one of you
It is in the way you carry yourself
With the graceful exterior
That completely conceals
The turbulence
That lies just beneath the surface
It is in your putting everyone else
Before yourself
It is the strength you possess
To birth a child one day
And the very next day
You're up at the crack of dawn
Tackling countless problems
Because life must go on
I am you and you are me
It is in the heartwarming joy
We feel as we own our strength
And yes
It is in the heartwrenching pain we feel
At societal glare
As they stare

And don't see us
All they see is a gender
And fair game
But I see you
YOU!
Yes, I see you
And you see me
You are me and I am you
And so on this day
I think of you

As much as we celebrate
The foremothers and foresisters
Who have finally
Shattered the glass ceiling
We want to pledge
To continue fighting for you
Because
What is a glass ceiling
If you are denied the right to live?
What is a glass ceiling
If you have no autonomy
Over your own body?
What is a glass ceiling
If they can snatch you
And cut off your holy of holies
Just because . . . ?
What is a glass ceiling
In a world where you can be sold
To the highest bidder
Or the lowest bidder for that matter

To do with you as they choose
Because you are a woman?
What is a glass ceiling
When you have no right
To an education?
What is a glass ceiling
In a world where you can
Be gifted to a man
As though you were property?

And so yes!
This Women's Day
We pledge to continue the fight
That was started
So many years ago
So that women all over the world
From Afghanistan to Zimbabwe
Will be seen first and foremost
As human beings

And when that day dawns
There'll be no more glass ceilings
To shatter
For that ceiling will now be the pavement
Upon which you tread
From which you sprint
And from which you'll soar
As high as your heart desires
Woman!
I salute you!

RECLAIM YOUR POWER

This is the place
Where it all began
The city where I came of age
In the darker corridors of life
The place where I was caged
Forced to deny myself
To become a shadow
Of the woman I once was
This place where I learned
All is not always as it seems
The place where
My voice was silenced
Movements restricted
Connections canceled
Past deleted
Future denied
Present confiscated
Confused
How did I get here?
Growth stunted
Opinions rejected
Freedom? What freedom?
Accused

Defamed
Maligned
Scandalized
Yes—they're synonymous
Needed to say it twice
Heard the accusations
Felt the chains
The shame was never mine
Day in, day out
Till the days became months
And the months years
And still I persevered
I will not cancel this place
Where I was burned
And oh, was I torched!
I thankfully learned
You can be
Rejected and dejected
And also elevated by sheer willpower
Anybody can cancel you
That's part of life
When you cancel yourself though
That's the tragedy
They can't get to you
Without your permission
The power is in your hands
To take back your life
And so from the ashes
I rise and soar
To heights I had never imagined

This is the future
I forged for myself
Polished and refined
Against all odds
Here I am
In this place
Where I encountered my strength
Hello HOUSTON!

The Walk to Freedom

Out walking this morning
And I start thinking
There are various walks you can be on

Some walks take a really long time
Sometimes it takes ages to realize
You need to take that walk
The walk to self-discovery is a must
Don't postpone it until it's too late
Take that walk when you still have time
To enjoy the authentic you
That you are bound to discover
I do not regret my walk to self-discovery
Instead, I wish I'd taken it sooner
This walk!
That led me to this place of freedom
                                                            And of joy
                            And truth
                                        And endless possibilities
I am never retracing my steps

Take that walk
I pray you find that which uplifts you
And improves the world

Make Your Heart Whole Again

Don't just cover those wounds
Heal them from the inside out
Or they will become your aura
They will fester
And stink
And stain
And choke everything
And everyone you touch

Expose IT
To the healing powers
    Of light
                  And truth
                                And time
                                And tears

Let the truth unveil it
The tears cleanse it
The light purify it
And let time heal it
When healing is complete
The anger the hurt
And the pain will be gone
All that's left is gratitude

And truth
And hope
And life!
And you can live again
And hope
And share
And dream
Wholeheartedly!
Make that heart whole again
And until you heal it
Don't give it
And when you're ready
May love find you

The Loudest Silence

A very cold day today
Too cold for the outdoors
So instead
I stay indoors and just enjoy
The warmth and love inside

It is freezing outside
Yet toasty inside
So my mind wanders off
And I think of all the great surprises
That you'll find
If you dare to live!
These make life such an adventure

In my trials and triumphs
I have been amazed to discover
In the times of my deepest oppression
I found my liberation
And it was at my weakest
That I found my strength

My bravery came roaring out
From my deepest fear

And in my very sorrow
I found my joy

The gates to freedom
Were right there
Within the confines
Of my captivity
All I had to do
Was look

My silence was loud
The loudest I've ever been
I was deliberate in my silence
The guilty heard me
Loud and clear
And behold
In my silence
I found my voice

So as you journey through life
Remember that all you seek
Is buried deep within you
All you need to do
Is to want it from the depths of your soul
And you'll find it

Happy searching!

An Invitation

And the elements
They whispered to my soul
Come here
Where the birds once sang
Come to the place
Where the river once flowed
And the trees stood in full glory
Come to the place
Where the sun
Gave you its radiance
And warmth
And life
Come closer
To this barren land
Bare and quiet
Cold and damp
Behold the beauty
For it is still there
In a different form
Beauty nonetheless
Look for it
If you know how to look
And behold its glory

Tread lightly
For beneath your feet
And all around you
Nature sleeps
To awaken again
In all its splendor
Tread lightly but come thither
This too . . .
Is worship
Gloria in Excelsis

O My Soul

(Birthday praise)

If my soul were an engine
Nature would be the fuel
That powers it
If my soul were troubled
The sky would be the blue
That calms it
If my soul were somnolent
The chirping of these winged ones
Would be the hymn
That stirs it into wakefulness
If my soul were a flute
The wind would be the lips
That bring forth an endearing tune
If my soul were a guitar
These twigs would be the fingers
That strum it
My soul was held captive once
Your rays came through
Like blazing shards
At the same time illumining all
And breaking up
The chains of captivity

I bask in the rays of your light
As I walk in the beauty of creation
And all that's in me
Comes to life

Let all that is in me
Love, adore, and bless your creation

Broken Yet Whole

Something about this place
Just something
I step into the light
But expect the darkness
To overtake me
And consume me
And confound me
The light persists
I bask in its glow
And I realize
The glow is coming from me
From deep within
It can't be put out
It's always with me
It starts from the inside
Spreads outward
Very slowly
Soaking every fiber
Of my being
Transforming me
And everything around me
Resplendent
I open the door wider

More light
No pain
No fear
No doubt
Dare I hope?
I close my eyes
The tears course down my face
Through the tears
I see a thousand shimmering lights
I smile
Broken yet whole

I can breathe
I breathe
I hope
Here I am again
Houston!

Presenting: Me

I don't think of what people notice
When they look at me
If I were to guess . . .
Maybe it is my complexion
Black
Ebony
Coffee
Please keep the cream

Maybe it is my hair
Short tight black curls
With a touch of gray
You might call it kinky
I call it my hair!

It could be my eyes
Which have seen a lot
And yet reveal so little
Until you dare to really look
It could be my smile
Which lights up my entire face
Transforming my countenance
But sometimes refusing to reach my eyes

Or could it be my wrinkles
Earned from both mirth and dearth
Maybe it is my voice
Sometimes soft, gentle, hesitant
And even shy
And yet strong, assertive, engaging!

It could possibly be my ample bosom
Slightly drooping
And why not?
It has helped sustain
Two young beautiful lives
Maybe it is my hips
Which are of childbearing proportions
Or is it my derrière
That sashays gently
Left then right
As if responding to some inaudible music
One might want to tarry there a little
For there, too, I am endowed
But nay, nay!
I am no seductress
So I bring you back to that which matters
My eyes!
Through which you can behold my spirit
I will show you the humanity
The love and joy and kindness
Faith and gratitude
And determination
That rule my life

If I cared about how you see me
I would be opening myself
To your cultural standards
Your expectations
Your bias
Your judgment

You WILL see me for who I am
Or you will not see me at all!

Finding the Mountaintop

The descent from the mountain
Down into the valley
Takes no effort
One little slip
One wrong turn
And you careen down
At the speed of light
Breakneck speed
Hitting rock bottom
In no time flat

To ascend from the valley though
Now that takes guts
It takes determination
And recognition
That you do not belong
In the bottomless pit
The knowledge that you have the power
To change the story

On my way up from the valley
I reached a place of forgiveness
And I exchanged that for my anger
I reached a place of love

And there I left my hate

I exchanged my despair for hope
And realized I had left the burden of fear
Somewhere along the way
At the same place where I found joy
I found laughter and strength
This is a great place to be

And as I look down from the mountaintop
Down to the valley below
I contemplate the darkness
I left behind
And to my great delight, I find
That in my ascent
I had climbed higher than I had been
Before the fall

And as you read my redemption story
May you be encouraged
To make your way out of the valley
It is a tough climb
But well worth it
And as you climb
Be sure to drop the weight that holds you down
Hate and fear and pain and despair and anger
That's what keeps you in the valley
Make that climb
Find your mountaintop
I wish you great success

OUT OF DARKNESS

To come from a horribly dark past
And become a point of light for others
Takes more than grace
It takes guts!
The guts to look back and take stock
To look at where you've been
And promise yourself
"Never again!"
Never again will I take that path or lead someone down that abyss

Never!

It takes presence of mind
To know that
You are NOT what happened to you
It takes a kind heart
To say, "This ends with me, and it ends now"
It takes love to stretch out your hand and say, "Here, I'll share my light with you"

Conquer that past
Become the point of light for someone
There's too much suffering

In the world
Be the point of light
For as many as possible
And lead them out of darkness

All Hurt the Same

Woke up to some music
Feeling all teary
It is the melody
And the soulful beat
The haunting sound of the vocals
And the words
That I interpret
And I weep for the artist
For the sadness his song evokes
Oh, how he must have hurt
Oh, how I wept
And moaned
And sighed
And realized
It is not for him I cry
For I, too,
Have walked this path
I cry for him
As I cry for me
The tears intermingle
The pain becomes one
And before long
I am crying for humanity

For whether we know it or not
We are all the same
We hurt and bleed
The same

And now
It is time to heal
And still
I sigh
I know . . . it takes time

Cocoon

I was made bold
And beautiful and blessed
The Maker of the universe
Took away my tears decades ago
Completely dried up the well
He knew what great sorrow lurked ahead
Yet to be unveiled
He strengthened me in readiness
In place of these tears He took

He gave me an excess of joy
An abundance of peace
So when the years of sadness came
The joy would outshine the sorrow
And burn it all out
The peace would completely engulf me
And keep me safe
Wrapped as though in a cocoon
Untouched, unharmed, unscathed
By the sorrow that surrounded me
I was in the center of this sorrow
But was able also to be on the outside
Looking in like a spectator

Spectacular!
Surreal!

The sorrow became easier to bear
And inconsequential even
Looking back
I see that at my weakest
I was my strongest
The years of sorrow are over
Do not be saddened
By my story
Instead, rejoice with me
As I tell you of my redemption
I survived
I thrive
Magnificat!

Your Garden, Your Shears

When the vines
That pull you down
Hold you back
And choke you
The vines of greed
And abuse
And hatred
And gender
And culture
And deception
Those vines!
When they've overtaken you
And you're tempted
To believe all is lost
Don't!
There comes a day
When you grab the shears
And get to work
Cutting off the vines
Removing the chaos
Restoring order
Reclaiming what's yours
Some of the branches will be broken

They've been pulled
In the wrong direction
For far too long
Some of the branches
Will be dead
They were not strong enough
To withstand the negative force
Some is lost
But all is not lost
Do not mourn
Do not regret
There was a reason
You went through the darkness
Now you're in the light
Grow, child, grow!
The time to heal has come
It is time for that comeback!
Sis
Do you need my shears?

Symphony of a Million Leaves

I was made
For days such as this
With the brilliance of the sun
Shining through all dark crevices
Making all things bright and new
Giving me some time to just be!
And its heat with loving caresses
Giving rise to sensations
Long forgotten
Rejuvenating and regenerating
And just when you think
It's as bright as it can be
It gets even brighter
Glorious!
I was made
For winds such as these
That blow through a thousand trees
With the resulting symphony
Rising from a million leaves
As they blow the heat away
Cooling the scorched earth
Underneath my feet
I was made for love such as this

That envelops me
In a firm embrace
Reminding me
That I am cherished
And treasured
And that this is my place
And that the world is mine too
To explore
And cherish
And preserve
And improve
I was made for a painful time
Such as this
To reach out to a hurting world
And touch someone
Telling him
You are loved
You matter
This world is yours too
I was made for a time such as this!

An Ode to Nature

My love wakes me up
In the wee hours of dawn
With an all too familiar serenade
I long to enjoy the music
But I want to enjoy
The semiconsciousness of sleep
And just as I reconnect
With my dreams
My love returns
In the form of rays
That slither silently through the cracks
Once more illuminating my world
Pulling me from the abyss
Into the light
Pulling me out to explore
That which is so freely given
To take in a world
That is never truly dark
If we know how to use
Our inner eyes
And once again
I'm outdoors
Exploring that which I have explored

A thousand times
And yet
I feel as though this is the first time ever
Pure joy!
Gloire à Dieu

DARKISH THOUGHTS

Flood my mind this morning
Interrupting a beautiful walk
So I pause on my favorite park bench
To let the memories flow
So I can purge
And experience the catharsis
That I so often get through writing
Thoughts of a time
When my freedom was taken
My speech, too, was taken
And my laughter left me
Of its own free will
For there's no real laughter
Where there's no freedom
There were no tears either
And I finally understood
That the absence of tears
Does not indicate the presence of joy
I still hear the accusations
The rules and regulations
And above all, the threats
Are you trying to kill me?
Because my mere existence

My very happiness
And self-direction is a threat to you?
And the more ominous
I will DO something!
Would send a shiver
Down my spine
I hear the echo of the threats
Even now as I pause in this park
Now, it is just a hollow sound
And I am thankful that I have my voice
And my laughter
And my freedom
Gives you an inkling
Of why I love the outdoors
So vast, so beautiful
So liberating
With endless possibilities
I could not live my life for myself
What gives you the right
To live your life
And live mine too
Heck NO
There are various kinds of prisons
Sister, yes, you and you too
Do not accept a life of bondage
You owe yourself the duty
To break free

A Recipe for Renewal

You have been given this ability
To renew your spirit
And heal yourself
An ability that many do not recognize
Is an integral part of being
Take a seemingly horrific day
Lots of disappointments
Your goal just beyond your grasp
Cries of regret
Groans of despair
Now try this:
Throw in a little sunshine
Lots of laughter
A splash of color
A little piece of the heavens
The wind on your back
And on your face
And in your hair
The rays of the sun gently stroking your skin
Kissing you most delightfully
Glorious moments with loved ones
There you go!
Now you are praying the day never ends

And you find yourself thanking God
For yet another perfect day!
That's you healing yourself
The woes of the morning are forgotten
You are ready to start afresh
That is power!
Enjoy it!

The Sword over My Head

The sword that held me captive
The sword that was wielded over my head
The sword that rendered me powerless
That sword!
Let me tell you something
About that sword!
There comes a time
You have to look the threat in the face
Know that what resides in you
Is greater than the external force
That keeps you imprisoned for so long
When the day of triumph came
That sword lost its power
It fell and shattered into tiny pieces
I sashayed over the pieces
In my fine dainty heels
Every step taking me closer to freedom
I picked up the broken pieces of the sword
And smiled when I realized
It was not steel
It was not even glass
It was like cotton in my hand!
Powerless!

Let me tell YOU something
Don't hide your fierce!
When faced by your fears
Confront the weakness that oppresses you
You are much stronger than your oppressor
Don't roll over
Fight!

On Contemplating Joy

I have contemplated life itself
On this path
Today my mind considers
That which is in the human Spirit
The Spirit that dwells in us
For me it permeates every fiber of my being
I am soaked in it
And it drips from my soul
Like rivers of water
It touches others
It gives calm and restores peace
And hope
And delight
It is a stream that flows from within
And you couldn't hide it
If you tried
You can't conceal it
It is a gift to share with others
With whom you walk upon this journey
Today, I contemplate
Joy that you cannot explain
The joy that keeps you going
Even in perilous times

The joy and hope that will motivate you
To extend goodwill
To those who need it the most
These birth a resilience
The resilience which is in the center
Of the human experience
As we walk into each new day
Look at fear in the face
And look deep within you
Look within your circle of support
Our souls are linked
In a fierce circle
A circle of fire
That will defeat the darkness
That hangs over you
Remain steadfast!

We Will Be Glorious Again

I take my cues from nature
Trees remain standing
No matter how harsh the winter
All we see is the outward appearance
The sheer determination to survive
That which goes on underground
Is left to the imagination
The lush green leaves are gone
Some of the branches will be lost
Because it is hard to sustain the whole
But the roots are hard at work
To remain standing
If the tree will just remain standing
If you will just remain standing
At the end of winter
The tree is again glorious
Victory lies ahead
If we don't give up
The time to fight is now

The Raging Fire of Hope

Darkness hangs over the earth
Much like a forboding
Bringing dearth and fear to all
Death to everything without hope
Darkness has a powerful hold
Only if you let it
Behold, the sun bursts through
Parting the darkness
Much like the parting of the Red Sea
When this happens
We smile and know
There's a bigger force at work
The rays of the sun
Pierce through the darkness
The darkness loses its power
It becomes patchy
Scattered
Just a memory of itself
It loses its hold over you
The fear is gone
Suddenly a dark day
A gloomy life
A miserable existence

Is resplendent with light
Life and hope and joy!
The life that is only possible
In the magical power of light
The raging fire of hope

Happy Women's Day?

Happy Women's Day?
I don't know about that
I am certain of one thing
There's a lot of work to be done
Today, as you celebrate Women's Day
Several women are getting killed
By their "dear" husbands
Because they are women
As you celebrate, a lot more are getting raped
By friend and foe alike
And please do not forget
By brother
And uncle
And cousin
And father too!
Because they are women
Even as you raise your champagne glasses
Young girls are turned into Trokosi
To be owned by a man
And become a perpetual slave
To satisfy the lust, whims, and caprices
Of the all-important man
Till the end of their days

They are raped and beaten
Debased and dehumanized
Because they are women
And please take note
This becomes their fate
Because of a crime committed by a male relative!
As you put on your dancing shoes
Young girls are being mutilated
Because of course they are women
They have no rights over even their own vaginas!
As you celebrate Women's Day
Young and not-so-young girls
Are sold and turned into sex slaves
Because they are women
Please, as you toast each other
Remember the women
Who cannot leave their abusive husbands
Because you all say they cannot leave
They cannot live
Because they are women
Please don't forget
The young girls who are force-fed
So they can be fat
So they can attract a man!
Because they are women
And fatter women are more enjoyable during sex
A pox on you and your cruel culture!
You all celebrating
Whatever you do, don't forget them
As you dance

Don't forget the women
Who are accused
And haunted, hunted, and killed
Because their husbands died
That, too, is the woman's fault
As you celebrate
Remember: being born a woman, Black, and poor
Is just the circumstance of your birth
Accepting what society forces on you
Now that's the tragedy
Dammit!
Get out of this complacency
And fight for your rights
ENOUGH!

Transform

Razor-sharp
Hard as rocks
I hear the crackle and crunch under my feet
Like glass shattering
Breaking the silence of the morning
I look down and behold the snow
Which just yesterday was as soft as the clouds
Snowman- and snow castle-worthy
Today, this same snow
Is like a weapon
Sharp, hard, rock-solid
Swords and shards
Jagged-edged
Dangerous!
Could be part of an arsenal
Weaponry
To fight, maim, and kill
The drop in temperature
Was the agent of transformation
Adversity, much like the cold
Will sharpen us
It will refine us
And strengthen us

Transform us
And prepare us for greatness
If we understand the process
And have faith
Don't bow
Rise!

What Was and What Will Be

I save lots of treasures
In my archives
And when the days are gloomy
I feast my eyes
And nourish my soul
On what was
And what will be
If I give it time
So should you
In your darkest moments
When you think the darkness
Will overpower you
Hold on to that fire
Carefully hidden in your soul
It is always there
Guard it jealously
Don't ever lose that light
Don't let the hope die
For that tiny ray of hope
Will lead you out of your despair
And guide you out of the darkness
Lighting your way

To a great tomorrow
Hold on, sis
Don't let go
All will be well

Shadows

Shadows from the past
Come crawling from the pages of the book
Suddenly darkness falls
Covering a very joyful morning
And just as the sun is still present
Even when covered by a cloud
So, too, does the joy remain
Behind the shadows of sadness
I have to get rid of this darkness
So I walk in worship
I walk in His garden
And raise my hand to the heavens
As I remember His promises
That He will never leave me
Or forsake me
I believe His word
As I gaze upon His beautiful creation
And have assurance
That His word is true
I take comfort in His word
The promise in His word
Gives me strength
I renew my strength

My resolve
And I find my joy
Ahh
The healing power of Grace

YOU WILL THRIVE!

When you begin to lose faith in humanity
When you fail to see the beauty
And you consider man's unkindness
And you are about to give up
Please don't!
Step out of your cage
Step into nature
Take a deep breath and . . .
Consider the fish in this frozen lake
They are not dead
They are alive
They will thrive again once the winter is over
Behold the trees
They have lost all their glory
They look like all is lost
But . . .
In a few short months
They will regain their beauty
Let me introduce you to this beauty of a garden!
It has retained its beauty
In spite of the harshness of the weather
Everything else is under the snow
But these trees . . .

They have put the snow to good use
They use it to adorn their branches
And enhance their beauty
The gray skies of today
Will be gone tomorrow
In their stead will be brilliant skies
At the sight of which
You will catch your breath
And say
How glorious!
So when you hurt
You feel mistreated
And defeated
And you're about to give up
Please don't!
You will overcome
YOU WILL THRIVE!
If the rest of creation can do it
So can you

BLESSINGS IN STILLNESS

Each day brings blessings
If we are intentional
In looking for them
We do find them
If we see the big picture
Yesterday was gloomy
So I looked harder
Listened more keenly
For the blessings it held
I walked two miles
In search of something meaningful
The sun did not make an appearance
The sky was gray
The snowbanks were waist-high
The birds were silent
Not a rustle from the leaves
Even the trees were bent over
As though in reverence
I noticed the stillness around me
There was no wind
Nothing
I listened to the sound of the silence
It seemed as though God had spoken

To his creation, He said
Be still and know
The wind was still
The birds were still
The trees stood silent
Who am I
Compared to the wonder
That is the cosmos?
Reverently
I stood still
And I knew
And . . .
I know

Change Your Story

Just announced to my mates
It is twenty-three degrees and uncharacteristically warm
For this time of year in Minnesota
As I complete my two-mile walk
I realize I shouldn't have layered up
I am sweating!
Me!
From the forest
Coastal region
At the foot of Mount Fako
Usually warm
Sometimes unbearably so
Hot mostly!
Gets me thinking
Human beings can adapt to anything!
Thank goodness we have the minds
To choose what to adapt to
Do not for any reason
Adapt
To ill treatment
Suffering
Abuse
You know your pain

Do not adapt to that!
Your battle determines your weaponry
Get up
Fight
Change your story
Write your story!

Fears Are Just Memories

Out on my favorite trail
Enjoying a great walk
Not too cold at fourteen degrees
The scenery fades to the background
As the past inserts itself
Apparently, there are thoughts
From a painful past
My mind has decided what we will dwell on
My mind has a mind of its own
She tells me often
Don't hide from memories
Don't refuse to think of the past
Just because it was painful
Bring it out
Stare it in the face
Eventually it loses its power over you
Don't try to forget it
Dwell on it until it is powerless
Becomes insignificant
I bow to her greater wisdom
Reach deep into the recesses of my mind
Pull up memories that were once painful
Very painful

I take them in my palm
Examine them one after the other
They are just memories
No fear
No pain
No sorrow
Just stuff
I crush them
They become dust in my palm
That I spread on the snow around me
It doesn't even have the power
To alter the color of the snow
Powerless!
I smile
Feel the joy in my heart
How could I not be joyful at the thought
Of a painful past
That made me understand
The power of kindness?
A past that made me gentle
Soft
Yet strong
Graceful
Grateful
For all who stood by me
A past that made me aware
Of my incredible strength
A past that brought out the lion in me

Women the World Forgot

Trampling and trudging down the trail
Thoughts turn tumultuous toward the Trokosi
The forgotten women
The world over
Thoughts roam angrily
To all women who suffer abuse
They suffer violence
Thoughts roam to women whose lives are taken
Because they are women
Thoughts roam to women
Who are considered a fraction of a man
Not because they are unintelligent
Not because they are uneducated
Not because they are poor
Not because they are not productive in society
They are women
So they are not worthy
These same women who gave you life
They birthed you!
And yet are not worthy to live as humans
Because they are women
It would be laughable
If it were not so infuriating!
Plodding and pounding the pavement
As if to pound some sense into this senselessness

I examine your excuses
It has always been this way
That is how the society is set up
It even says so in the Bible
Have you really read the Bible
Did that same society not say
Your entire race was not worthy
Did they not own you
Didn't they put a monetary value on your life
Didn't they choose who lived and who died
Were you not treated like chattel
You think they were wrong
But oh, hold up
You think what they told you about women is right?
That they should be treated like property
That they should become your punching bag
That their bodies are yours to do with as you please
That they should not be allowed a life
Oh, I see how it is
When you are part of the downtrodden
Then justice and fairness must be served
But when the rules favor you
Hallelujah! This is great!
I pray the day comes
When you grow a conscience
And become a human being
Maybe, just maybe
You'll be half as amazing
As the women you look down on
The same women who brought you forth!

Castaway

Once again!
The city of my entrapment
Has become the symbol
Of my freedom
Where at first
I was cast away
Into the ocean
With only a basket for a boat
Huge weight around my neck
Fighting and gasping
for every breath

Now I feel
Like a castaway
On an island
The weight around my neck
Is gone
I am free to chart my own course
And breathe
And be!
It took fourteen years
Of knotting
Now in the fourth year

Of the unraveling
I see the light
At the end of the tunnel
This light
Is a promise
I look forward to where it leads

LOVE IS LIFE ITSELF

And he said to me
"You think you are important
But remember
The hillsides of the world
Are full of festering corpses
Of people who once thought
They had it all."

And I said to myself
Yes, all living beings
Come to that certain end
It is a part of the cycle of life!
But, this ominous threat over my head
How is it different from death?
What kind of living
Can one experience
When the constant fear
Of the abuser carrying out his threat
Becomes part of one's reality?

People often ask
Why did she leave?
It was an empty threat

He was just angry!
But how do they know it was an empty threat?
What does a real threat sound like?
What does it look like?
And if it was indeed an empty threat
Is the fear it evokes any less real?
Is the inability to live a productive life
Any less real?
Is the insecurity you feel any less real?
Is the fear you feel as you look over your shoulder
Any less real?
Is the thumping of your heart
That you can feel in your ears
Any less real?
And then, again, how do you distinguish
When the threat is real?
How about all the others
Who have died real deaths
At the hands of their abusers?
Must one wait until the deed is done
And then the world will say
Alas, the threat was real!

And if you stay
And he takes your life
These same people will say
Why didn't she leave?

Love does not promise death
Love does not bring death

Love gives life
For, love is life itself!
So as I looked at his written words
That threatened my very existence,
And I looked further down at the words
That proclaimed "one day we will all die,"
I stood up,
Wiped the tears from my face
Shrugged the fear off my shoulders
And I said
"But first, we live!"
And to you today, I say
But first, we live!

About the Author

Inez Nambangi is a domestic abuse survivor reclaiming her voice through writing. She writes nature poetry filled with heart and hope to empower others toward healing and freedom.

Her debut poetry collection, *But First We Live*, contains walking meditations, allowing readers to embark on their healing journeys alongside Inez herself.

Inez's writing combines her personal experiences with her unparalleled love and talent for the poetic arts.

About the Illustrator

Megan Rizzo, also known as Daisy, is a freelance artist, published illustrator, and new mom currently based in Ann Arbor, Michigan.

Daisy was born and raised in Detroit, Michigan, but recently lived in the San Francisco Bay Area. She loves creating bright and colorful illustrations that highlight women, especially black women. She also enjoys using her work to support nonprofit, educational, and social justice work, such as Shado Magazine, University of Michigan, Yeah Art!, and 826 Michigan.

www.ingramcontent.com/pod-product-compliance
Lightning Source LLC
Chambersburg PA
CBHW060032180426
43196CB00045B/2619